Different Like Daisy:
Featuring Daisy and the Misplaced Mutts

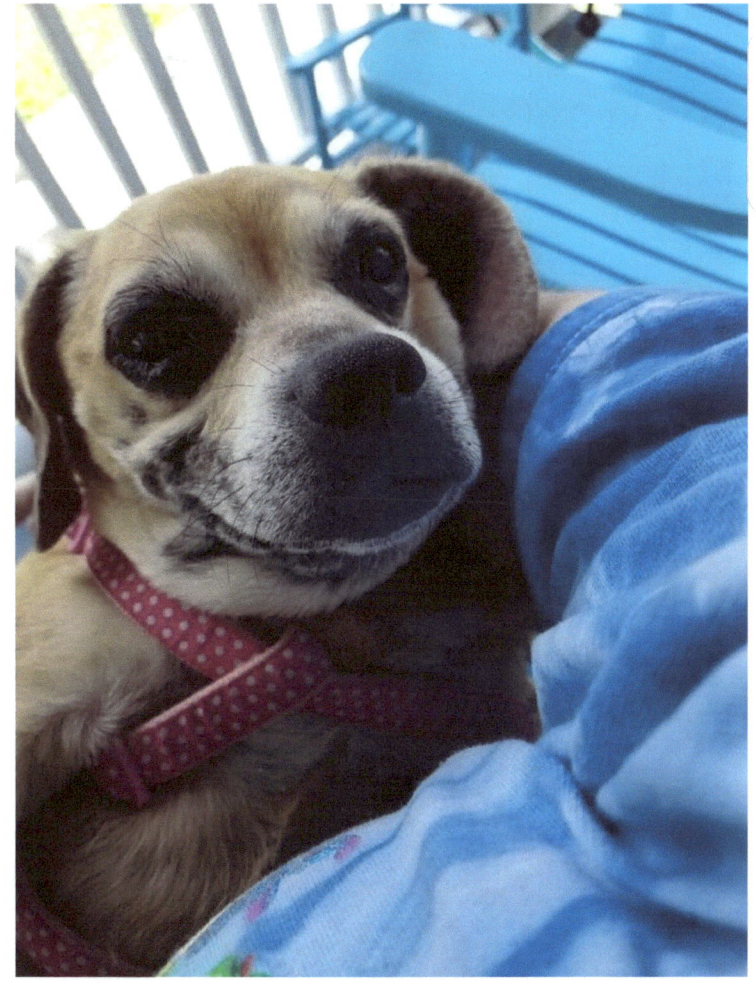

By Ann Carpenter

Did you know that pets could be different?
You and I don't look the same, either. We are all different, and that is ok!
Even if people, and dogs can appear different, we can still live our best life!
Let's take a look at some pets that look different, yet are living their best life:

Some are BIG

And

Some are small

Some, when rescued, have
Very little skin at all.

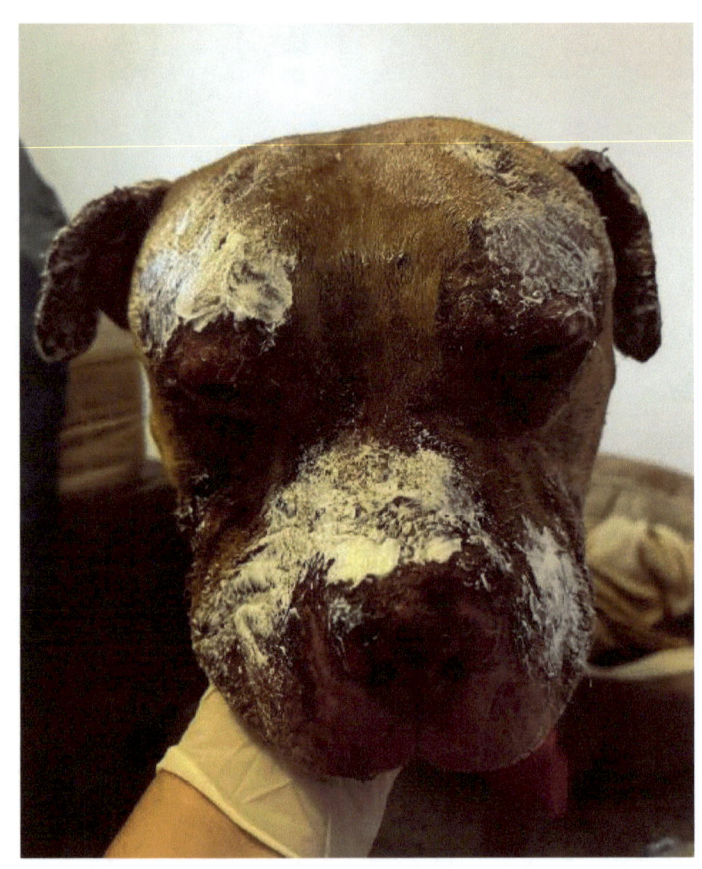

Dogs are so resilient….
This means they can overcome their challenges and differences. They do not let their differences stop them or define who they are.

Are you different than your friends or family?

Some dogs have funny teeth.
These funny teeth make them smile the cutest smile.
Can you smile and show your teeth?

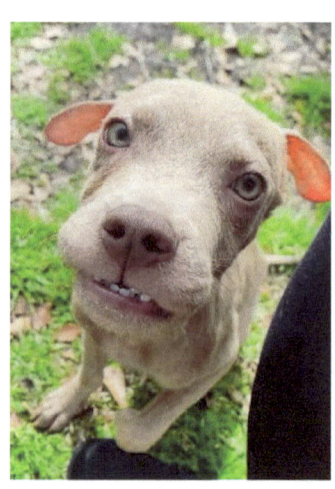

Some dogs have different colored eyes! Some are blind. Some are missing an eye.
Do your eyes look different than your friends or family's eyes?

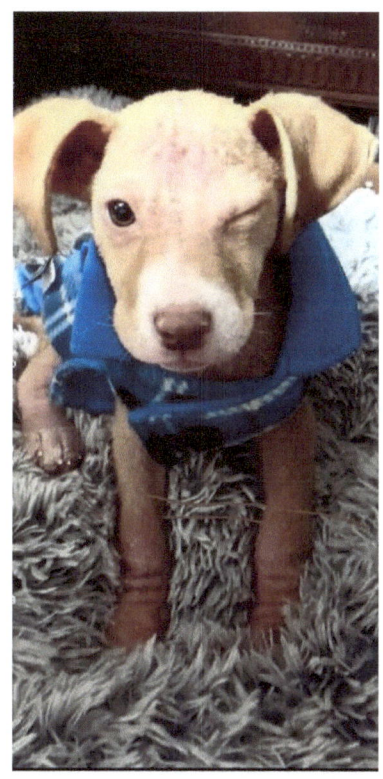

Some have different feet...
Are your feet different than your friends or family?
Are they bigger or are they smaller?
Have you ever hurt your foot and needed a bandage or a cast?

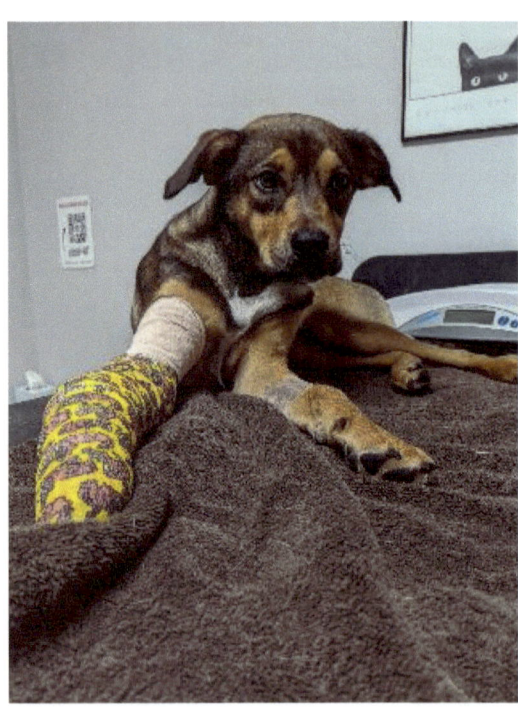

Now here is a different dog, I would like you to meet:

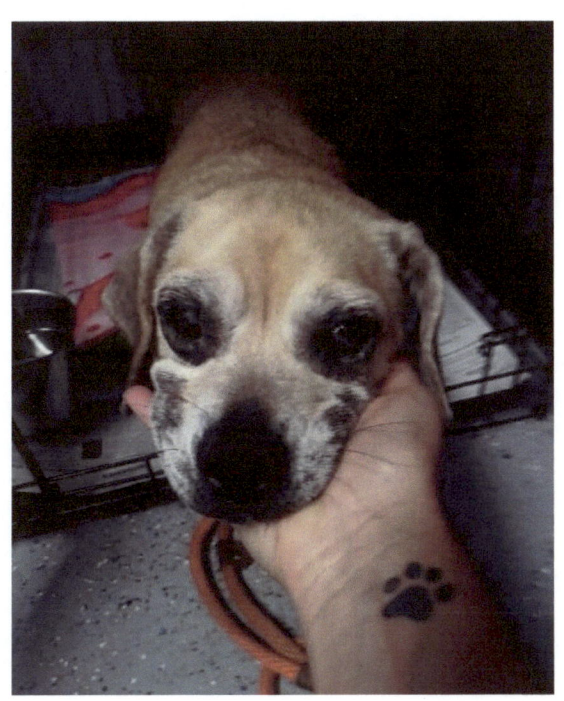

Daisy is allergic to certain foods. This means she cannot tolerate or eat these types of foods.

When she does eat these foods, it makes her skin itchy and it makes her skin look different.

Are you allergic to any foods?

Well, because certain foods make Daisy itchy and look different, her first family realized that Daisy needed more expensive food and more doctors' appointments and care so that she could feel better. However, this family was not able to afford the food that made Daisy feel better or the many doctors appointments which Daisy needed to go to. The family brought Daisy to an Animal shelter so that she could get a new family that could afford her food and doctor visits.

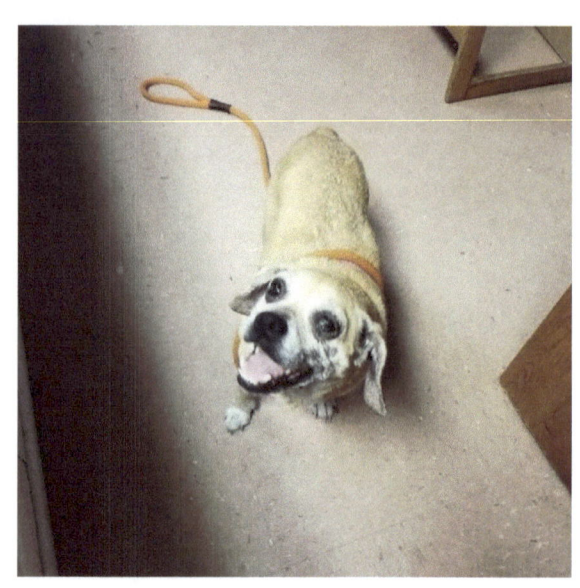

Her first family loved Daisy very much. They wanted what was best for Daisy. They also taught her several tricks. She could sit, lie down, play dead, and speak!

One day, Daisy met a new mommy. Daisy smiled in the car, before the car even left the animal shelter to bring her to her new home. Daisy was happy to have a new mom, and she knew that she would have the best life ever.
Being different is ok!

When Daisy arrived at her new home, she met Grandma Betty!
Daisy showed Mommy and Grandma Betty all her tricks that she knew.

Then, Daisy met her new sister and brothers! Their names were Ella, Jack and Rex!

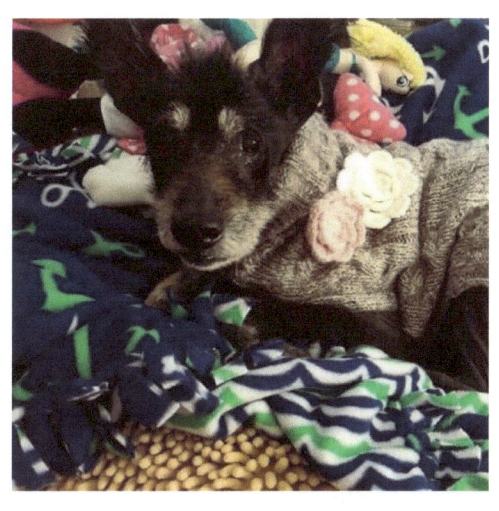

Then, Daisy got a new sister named Mouse. Mouse also looked different. She was very old. She was missing some fur and she was often cold, so Mommy put sweaters on sister, Mouse.
Mouse had also lived at the animal shelter, just like Daisy.

Then, Daisy got a new sister, Bella! Bella was also different. Bella needed a wheel chair to walk because her back legs did not work. Bella was also a rescue dog, Who was under the prior care of a doggy rescue organization called Misplaced Mutts.

Even though Daisy, her friends at the beginning of this book, and her new sisters all look different, they are all happy.
They are living their best life.
Daisy, especially, enjoys living her best life

Daisy loves playing dress-up!
Isn't Daisy silly?
Do you like to play dress-up?

Daisy loves going on walks to the beach.
Do you like to take walks?
Where do you like to walk?

Daisy loves going on a walk or stroller ride downtown, to see the boats on the waterfront.

Daisy loves puppy cups from the drive through restaurants. She gets puppy cups from the coffee shop or the ice cream shop.

Daisy loves to go on car rides!

Daisy loves going to her groomer to get a nice warm bubble bath!
The bath makes her skin feel all better!

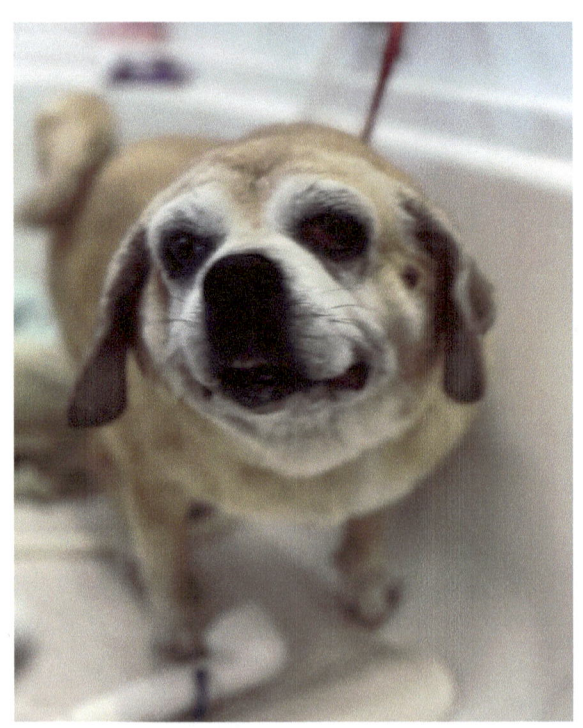

Daisy loves hugs…

…And Daisy loves kisses

Daisy loves a good nap in her cozy bed, every now and then! Do you ever take naps?

Daisy loves daisies!

But the thing that Daisy loves the most of all…

Is…..

SMILING

So let's all smile and be different, like Daisy!
Let's embrace what makes us different.
Let's treat everyone with respect and love, and accept that everyone is different!

½ of all proceeds from this book will go towards Misplaced Mutts, an amazing rescue agency in my small town here in North Carolina.

Misplaced Mutts is a wonderful organization, which saves the life of pets.

It is run by two incredible ladies, as well as many foster parents.